by Justin Dauer

www.the-culturebook.com
@the_culturebook

Copyright © 2017 Justin Dauer
Published by Lead Hand Books

Cover and book designer: Justin Dauer
Photographer: Justin Dauer
Illustrator: Bobby Price
Editor: Ann Maynard

ISBN: 978-0692840672

Contents

Foreword

We spend a third of our lives sleeping, and another third working. You can get better sleep by exercising, watching what you eat, and cultivating regular habits. But how can you get a better working environment? Succinctly and memorably, this book tells you.

I've worked many places during my long, serpentine career. Some places, you couldn't wait to leave. Others were like a sleepover at your favorite cousins' house. Some places make their workers feel valued, and coax brilliant work out of them like bees make honey. Other places, you'd feel justified quitting tomorrow and taking their clients with you.

What creates these different cultures and consequences? And how can you make sure your work environment brings out the best in everyone from day one? In this delightfully narrated and beautifully illustrated volume, Justin Dauer tells you all you need to succeed as a creator of great company culture.

Employers will learn how to end the problems that plague every organization—from failure shaming to lack of listening. You'll discover what to do on a new employee's first day to start the relationship off right. How to manage egos and expectations and create a level playing field for all. Why stepping away from your desk can produce unmatched insights. And how to build the kind of trust that results in better products and happier, more productive employees—employees who stick with you.

And Justin's text is just as useful for job seekers. You'll learn how to end an unhealthy work relationship and find your cultural match. How to win at interviewing; turn the job search into a journey that benefits you *and* your employer; and find the companies that are doing it right.

After reading this book, you'll know what's right and wrong at your place of business—and whether you can be part of the solution, or need to move on. It's the kind of knowledge that can save you years of wasted effort. Not bad for a book you can read in two hours.

During the past decade, designers and marketers have learned to cultivate empathy and make it part of the product development cycle. But we haven't applied the same empathy to ourselves, our colleagues, or our employees. Now we can. In the time it takes to fly from New York to Chicago, Justin Dauer will show you how to transform your life and our industry, one beautiful interaction at a time.

Jeffrey Zeldman
Founder, studio.zeldman

For Emmett, who fills my heart with so much love,
often I don't know what to do with it.

Introduction

It's Sunday evening. Another wonderful weekend is firmly under your belt. And yet, as you settle down into the couch, you're anything but content. There's that familiar feeling of dread in your stomach, uncomfortable and palpably inescapable. *Monday*. With the impending workweek looming large, events from the previous one replay in your head like an unwanted lowlight reel:

- The project review meeting in which your voice and feedback were disregarded entirely.
- The complete lack of energy and inspiration on your team, and from leadership, that ultimately compromised your end deliverable.
- The local half-day conference that you requested to attend, but were summarily denied. "You're needed in the office," after all.

The design field is largely comprised of talented, creative and passionate individuals and yet all too often the organizational culture in which we're expected to work—*to create*—stifles the very gifts for which we were hired. When the fire within someone gets extinguished, more than just their best work gets lost; they may burnout, leave their company, or switch fields altogether. The potential impact upon our industry is monumental. We as an industry are better than this—**and as human beings**, we deserve better too.

Whether you're in a leadership role wondering why your team seems miserable, or you're a passionate and dedicated designer dreading Monday, we can agree: a happy and well-supported employee is a fueled, charged, inspired creator. The quality of work is elevated, quality of life gets strengthened, and the organization itself becomes organically championed by the very people it supports. Our team members deserve nothing less— no matter the size of the company, the industry focus, or their particular role.

As someone who's long worked with and supported designers

and front-end developers in both design and tech-focused engagements, I've consistently seen how unhealthy internal cultures are tantamount to psychological abuse. How these environments have caused brilliant people to completely detach from their crafts and question why they pursued their paths in the first place. I've seen how they've impacted *my* passions, *my* work, and *my* ability to thrive. And I decided to do something about it.

Designers and front-enders have a unique advantage in solving the cultural problems that are sucking the life out of us. Several, in fact. The principles we will be discussing in this book derive from the perspectives and skillsets we already use daily: empathy, objectivity and, yes, ample creativity.

- Human-centered thinking drives our outward-facing work (user advocacy, usability, accessibility, the list goes on), so we will explore what happens when we turn that lens inward to address how to build trust and support.
- To designers specifically (though I'm speaking to front-enders as well), visual communication and successful design is built upon rules toward end-product success. There is no room for subjectivity in critique and project evolution. We'll discuss what happens when a similarly unwavering standard is in place to uphold *humble* leadership and allow talented people the freedom to do what they do best, without sacrificing the bottom line.
- We share the ability to (and I'll hate myself in the morning for using this term) "think outside the box" creatively: programmatically, or visually. It is our default setting, and it can propel us to seek out alternate forms of inspiration, or be amicable to adjusting their routines with the right tools. We'll be identifying those tools and how to implement them later in this book.

Creative cultures contribute to the resounding success of an organization and the work its team creates. They permeate the interactions at our office, the meetings we attend, and the manner in which we produce. It's very much about being focused on the human beings behind the projects and facilitating them doing their best work; getting there represents a shift in thought as much as in procedure.

The good news is we all can get there. Having said that, there's a journey to be had along the way to our destination.

I'm inviting you to join me.

CHAPTER

1

From
Square
One

/ 5

We create human-centered interactions and experiences in our field. Empathetic purpose drives our every decision. "Is this workflow intuitive?" "Does the level of contrast meet accessibility guidelines?"

Mobile First? In reality, it's *humans* first. This same mentality, turned inward, forms the cornerstone of something amazing: a creative culture.

A creative culture isn't felt in a company's home page elevator pitch, nor is it in the mission statement tacked to the wall of every cube. It isn't manufactured through after-hours beers with the team. It certainly doesn't grow out of "Hawaiian Shirt Day."

As we will discuss in this book, a thriving creative culture is the sum of many dynamic parts, and it is reinforced by organic interactions throughout the day. Its foundation is one of mutual respect, palpable and harnessed energy, and a complete commitment to its livelihood. Its impact is directly translated over to quality of work (no, I didn't misspell "quantity"), quality of life, and measurable performance.

The tone is set for an employee the moment they arrive for work on their first day.

Stepping Through the Door

The first day a new hire steps into their role is the organization's biggest opportunity for employee investment: welcoming them as a human being, rather than a "worker." The new hire's buy-in can hinge on whether they get treated like a passionate and driven individual or a paid ass in a seat—and they will be looking for cues throughout the day.

People feel vulnerable on their first day in a new role and a new company. Hell, in their first *month* there are all sorts of adjustments in play. The environment is foreign, the faces are fresh, and in large part, the way in which projects get tackled on the day-to-day has yet to be learned. A new-hire will be paying attention, logging away each detail and internalizing how they feel at each step. That first morning will communicate the organization's culture loud and clear. Is the employee welcomed at the door? Are they given a tour and introduced around? Or are they left to fend for themselves, setting up their workstation in silence? No one wants to feel lost or unwelcome.

It's safe to say we've all experienced both ends of the reception spectrum on our previous first day(s) on the job, successful or otherwise. For example, at one company I previously worked with, I was put into a client deliverable within the first five minutes of laying eyes on my desk. At another, my arrival was a surprise to everyone besides the person who hired me. And that person didn't show until 2:00 PM.

Alternatively, when an organization has a system in place to welcome a new employee (and not just onboard them), there can be magic. Best of all, designers and developers are uniquely equipped for doing precisely that.

For a moment, let's consider why we create personas in user experience design: to simulate the goals, desires, and thought processes of an individual, so as to better inform how they would accomplish a set of tasks. What do they want? How do they feel as they're progressing through that workflow? So now let's translate that general methodology—putting ourselves in the shoes of others—over to our wide-eyed new-hire's Day One experience.

A person on their first day wants to feel welcomed.
Flowers left on their desk, along with a handwritten welcome note.

A new employee would like to have easy access to logistical knowledge.
On that same welcome note, a URL to a landing page of helpful information. Slack credentials, email set-up, upcoming events, a list of restaurants in the area, etc.

Placing ourselves in the mindset of how someone feels comes back to the adage we learned in our formative years: **treat others how you'd like to be treated.** The Golden Rule will serve us well in this book and beyond.

So as you walk through the new hire's user experience, ask yourself: Does it match the story our organization tells everyone else?

When Story Meets Reality

A company tells its brand story to connect to its users, to keep them engaged, and to build relationships. How the organization came to be. Why its employees are charged to come into the office daily. Why they offer the products or services they do. It's also safe to say this brand story was communicated to the new hire multiple times, from the job description to the interview to the offer that brought them across the office threshold.

Story meets reality the moment a new hire walks through the door on Day One. For a new employee, all the positive momentum of signing on the dotted line and the perceived thrill of doing inspired work can live or die upon what happens next.

Now, whether or not you're a fan of Apple, it can't be disputed that they're one of the most powerful and influential brands on planet Earth. Full disclosure: I am one of the world's most foremost Apple fanboys (it's a self-proclaimed title). So I was quite intrigued to learn how they infuse their brand into their Day One. Taking place "always on a Monday," as Adam Lashinsky notes in his book *Inside Apple*, new employees are given a heap of branded welcome package merchandise, shiny new hardware, and a free lunch. As an outside observer: nothing too surprising there.

Lashinsky goes on to note that a new employee is expected to connect their new Mac to the company network completely unaided. By and large, if you've made it through the hiring process as an Apple advocate, it's assumed you have the chops to handle that tech hurdle yourself. Otherwise, the intent is to organically get you to connect with other employees and establish a dialogue.

Lastly, "an informal 'iBuddy' system provides the name of a peer outside the primary team who can serve as a sounding board, someone for the bewildered new employee to ask questions," he notes. Within an organization with as many moving parts as Apple, it sounds like a great way to mitigate the feeling of being overwhelmed. Not casting a new hire into the sea of the unknown and acknowledging their humanity in the process is certainly a good thing.

From this fanboy's perspective, these elements align with the company's brand story: the individual over the machine, intuition meeting expertise, refinement meeting the unexpected, and so on.

But is that the best representation of the Apple culture? Hard to say with absolute certainty having not gone through the experience personally. It seems like fairly standard corporate first-day fare, plus or minus an "i" prefix. Personally, what I'm looking for in a Day One is an experience that validates that I've made the right decision in signing the contract; one that propels me into my new role with positive energy, and makes it crystal clear who my company is and what they stand for.

The New Day One

In the recent past, I found myself at a business with a culture that wasn't the best fit on some very core principles: unsupported, utilized as a dehumanized resource, and a workplace lacking any semblance of a healthy, creative culture. It became rather self-evident that it was time for a change. And so, despite having no other role lined up, I left.

I dedicated the next few months to reenergizing, refocusing, and taking on some solo design and programmatic work. Over this time, I put a great deal of thought into how I saw my career evolving, considering a full gamut of options. I love crafting with my hands; perhaps carpentry? I thrive in environments where I can help grow the talents of others; maybe teaching? My alma mater, The School of the Art Institute of Chicago, was a walkable distance from my neighborhood. Effectively, I was drilling down to the core of what my passions were, and where the most creative energy could be harnessed and utilized for the long term.

The core commonality from those thoughts was a love for building things, and surrounding myself with passionate brilliance. As the common thread throughout my career, that bloodshot tunnel vision ultimately led to a wonderful opportunity: building a design practice and creative culture from the ground up.

At Nansen, a Stockholm-founded digital agency, I was hired and welcomed by Swedish speaker, designer, and co-author of *Noded – The Untouchable Business*, Jaan Orvet. Our thoughts, approach, and mindset toward cultivating creative culture aligned in absolute perfect harmony. I'll be referencing his thoughts and our conversations throughout this book.

It was here at the fledgling Chicago branch of the company, upon a baseline of imported Swedish culture and egalitarianism supporting my every move, where the purest form of The New Day One was crafted. This cultural mindset derives straight from the Scandinavian concept of *Jantelagen* (or *The Law of Jante*), which effectively means that no one person is greater than anyone else. Having visited Sweden numerous times over the years, I've seen the success of the concept applied in a business setting. Moreover, humility and restraint saturate the culture of the entire country. It's a simple, human-centric viewpoint that has influenced the ideas in this book tremendously.

First Impression

Why do I care so much about an employee's first day? In reality, it's a micro-fraction of their entire career. The fact of the matter is this: the consideration a company gives to how an employee is welcomed and brought into the fold speaks volumes as to what lies ahead.

After the ink is dry and logistics discussed, I arrange with our new team member to start with us on a Friday. As with the Apple example, many of us have likely become accustomed to first day Monday's; the prevailing thought being that there are consistency and momentum inherent in a consecutive five-day workweek. And there is. That said, I'm looking for a different kind of momentum: one that's predicated upon time for reflection of the employee's first day experience, that only carrying through the weekend will supply.

What follows is a process that's as finely tuned as it is organic. There are no client deliverables or billable work on tap today. Instead, I've laid out a series of events designed to acclimate my new team member as a valued human being, brimming with ideas and creativity. Through **acclimation**, **conversation**, **inspiration**, and **reflection**, their Day One unfolds as follows:

Acclimation

The remainder of the first half of the day is setup and prep, both tangibly and perceptually. To the former, personalizing and configuring their laptop as they see fit, and working with the appropriate team members to secure licenses and install the tools they need, for example. Instead of operating out of a closed-door office or sitting leagues away, I'm seated at the same table as my team. Any questions that arise will come to all of us:

"What are we using for file archival?"
– Let me walk you through how we set that up.

"Are we using Git or TFS for source code management?"
– Our Front-End Lead, sitting right there, can best field that one.

And a dialogue has begun.

We'll take a look at the office space and see how others are currently working and utilizing the environment. Nothing is off the table; it's about wherever you can do your best work. On the couches, in the kitchen area, at a coffee shop. There's respect for the employee's process, and Orwellian eyes are not marking when people are walking out the door. It can take a few weeks (and maybe a brain cleansing) to erase a previous company's thought shackles from their minds, but this is how we operate.

Conversation

Up to this point, the Day One fare has been relatively straightforward. Our new hire has been acclimated with the team, the office space, and their workstation. Around noon I ask them to start winding down what they're doing, as it's time to head out for an off-site lunch. We won't be returning to the office today. The reactions I receive when I ask our new team member to pack up their things for the day range from a raised eyebrow to curious laughter.

Being ever mindful of a new employee's mindset on this first day, I ensure there's no logistical fumbling on the company's part: we head to a pre-selected, vetted restaurant. Over lunch, there's normal, human conversation. We've chatted a bit previously over the interview process, but now it's about getting to know this person as, well, a person.

"Hope you like this restaurant, it's one of my favorite places."

"Are you from the area originally?"

"Cubs or Sox?" (I don't care either way, but it's what Chicagoans ask one another).

Since the conversation evolves over bites of food, let's keep it casual, but focused on genuinely listening. Taking a team member out to lunch on their first day isn't rocket science; how they're engaged (constructive dialogue versus cell phone tunnel vision) is where we see the most value.

The end of the meal doesn't conclude our conversation, however. After lunch, I'll have a café on tap (Fɪɢ 1) that's conducive to having a seat, quiet enough for hearing one another speak, and serves up great coffee (a good pour will be another running theme in this book). This environment informs a more passionate discussion: on development, on design, on inspiration, on how our team functions within the organization, on current and future projects. The clock isn't watched, judging gazes aren't cast, and implications of seniority or hierarchy are left off the table. It's a small piece of the day, but the approach is directly representative of the creative culture they'll soon be thriving in.

The "inspiration" part of the discussion is no accident, either. It directly fuels the next part of our Day One.

Inspiration

With our bellies full and caffeine in our veins, there's only one

Fig 1: Pickwick Coffee Roasting, Chicago.

more expectation for the day.

"What inspires you in the city?", I'll ask.

The designer or developer's role is contextualized by digital endeavors. However, inspiration has no such limitations. As such, this isn't merely another conversation point: we physically go to wherever/whatever their answer yields. The Agora sculpture in Grant Park (Fig 1.1), the Tiffany Dome in the Chicago Cultural Center, and a craggy meditative stretch of Lane Beach in Edgewater (just north of downtown) have been some responses. My expectation, then, is to have them talk me through why [whatever it is] has inspired them. Understanding what has influenced them in that regard provides insight into their approach to visual or programmatic communication that transcends what folio work can yield.

The jaunt is more than a field trip, of course; it's a direct manifestation of the creative culture. This part of Day One can require some thoughtful guidance on behalf of the person driving the experience. It's a safe guess that this is like nothing the new employee has encountered before as part of their introductory experience, and opening their mind "on the spot" can be no small feat. In reality, it can be as simple as a stretch of road. Or a vinyl toy shop. Or a view of the city. If they get "stuck," we're not going to shrug and call it a day; I'll have some pre-selected inspiration spots ready to go, just in case.

In some instances, I've taken designers and front-enders to the Modern Wing at the Art Institute of Chicago to appreciate and discuss a broad swath of creative inspiration. Design and code are art, and analyzing another artist's communicative process in their gallery pieces is mutual fuel. By having me provide the venue for inspiration, a different, though no less engaging, dialogue and critique has evolved.

Reflection

At this point, a first day of copious amounts of healthy discussion (and coffee, and walking) has served to establish a tone of humanized dialogue and mutual respect. Again, direct representations of the creative culture they've signed up for. Their Day One has come to its conclusion.

By the business clock there's typically not much time remaining; as such, the remainder of the day and weekend can be taken for thought and reflection on what was, very likely, a first day unlike any other they've had before. In fact, it hasn't been uncommon for hugs, or even tears (the joyous kind), to turn up as we part ways. That is the exact momentum I want to be carried through a couple of days of rest and into Day Two the following Monday.

The new employee now goes into their weekend with a crystal clear sense of how I, and the company, value and respect them. How we appreciate that they trust us to support their passions and abilities from Day Two onward. You can't fake sincerity or human decency; two fundamentals that many companies are incapable of supplying.

Though I've crafted this onboarding experience through the lens of my team, I've worked with the other members of management to ensure it's been translated and applied to how we hire within all roles at all levels of the company.

Everyone Has a Seat at the Table

Value and respect. A human-centered approach to how employees are regarded has these ideals bound to the double helix of its DNA. It takes the first day occasion leagues deeper than lunch and a handshake by providing an experience that is directly personal over boilerplate. Everyone in the office should be afforded the opportunity of this Day One, as roles and seniority do not define the individual behind them.

Orvet speaks through the lens of Swedish culture when he cites precisely such a standard:

> *"It's ok to be a human; it's ok to be you. And on top of that, you can also be this role at the company where we work. It's always having the individual at the forefront."*

It's a matter of planning to make sure a team member's Day One is not just an uplifting experience, but also keenly representative of a truly creative culture. It's a matter of consistency and authenticity to make sure this carries through every single day-onward, organically.

Whether you're a designer or developer, client-side or service-side, internal or consultant, a baseline of intrinsic human decency, support, and talent development has to be established. Though this is a book written for designers and developers, these principles will lay the foundation for a healthy, supportive culture in any industry. As in design and development, there are beacons of those who are "doing it right" culturally whom we need to take a look at. In fact, that's where we'll go next.

2 / 5

A
Healthy
Dynamic

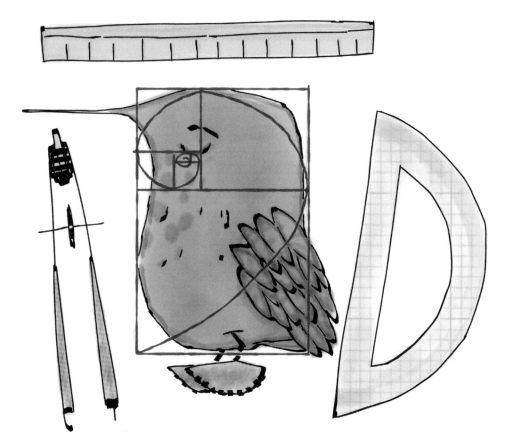

Let me tell you about Nick Sarillo, a pizzeria owner.

A fellow lifelong Chicagoan, Nick is the founder and owner of two aptly named restaurants, Nick's Pizza & Pub, both situated in the surrounding suburbs. He's the author of *A Slice of the Pie: How to Build a Big Little Business.* He's also been featured in *The New York Times, Inc. Magazine, FastCompany, The Economist,* and a dozen other publications. And, he's a TEDx speaker.

In fact, I could expound endlessly upon where he's been featured and the media attention he's received, but the beautiful thing at the source is *why* he's received so much exposure. This humble yet brilliant man has developed a system of belief, support, and development dubbed "trust and track," which is the core of his business' culture and operations. What this means is that he gives his team the tools to succeed and to help the business thrive, and then trusts them completely to do exactly that. In large part, Nick is putting his near 20-year-old multi-million dollar business' operations in the hands of local high school students. And they knock it out of the park, day in and day out.

Transparency and organizational flatness saturate every aspect of the business' culture and operations and form its foundation. In a tour of his Elgin location, Nick took me to the lower level of the facility where the company's full financial statements are tacked to the wall for all to see, updated daily. Everyone's current hourly wage is also listed on a whiteboard, and for those who haven't reached the salary level of their peers, the means to do so are listed on the same board. If you want to make more money, you train in more areas of the restaurant's operations. Nick and his leadership team happily support you to do so.

Employees are entrusted with developing individual units of the restaurant's operations and P&L—the bar, the restaurant floor, etc.—including forecasting and inventory management. The employees become so advanced at their craft that Nick's internal training program, Nick's University, has been made available to the public. Fortune 500 companies have sent C-level staff to attend the courses, which in actuality may be taught by a 17-year-old high school student.

Underpinning all of this is the culture of the restaurant, quite literally built into the walls. As Nick led me around, pointing out some areas of the facility he built with his own two hands (Fig 2), every member of the staff was on a first-name basis with him. And he knew everyone's first name in kind. I witnessed a symphony of team members operating in harmony, swiftly preparing different areas of service for the evening rush.

"We don't have a lot of rules. We're not commanding and controlling. We're actually saying, 'make your own decisions,'" he told me over a slice of pizza. "Why I'm passionate about getting this word out there—and how we can create great places to work in any organization—is I felt here I'm doing it in the restaurant business, which is typically thought of as a pass-through industry."

Trust in an employee, respect for their individual voice and support toward their growth are commendable core cultural qualities. Nick's team is charged and energized to come into work on a daily basis because the cultural match from the company's values (posted on a sign right in the lobby) to the individual's values is an exact fit. Openly shared and discussed during their interview process, those mutual passions and beliefs palpably carry through every day the employee walks through the door.

An environment in which collaboration and inspiration propel us forward is integral to achieving a common goal. Nick's example resonates, as it's these exact core values that have put them and their business's cultural model in the spotlight as a beacon.

No Place for Pride

Pizza parlor or Fortune 500 tech juggernaut, the cultural backbone of a business will falter unless it's built upon respect. It's a simple notion: put the employees, the very talent keeping the lights on, first.

Hand in hand with that understanding comes leveraging the power of humility.

I Bet You Think This Section is About You

The weight with which unhealthy relationship synergies can, and will, undermine team members' collective confidence is massive. A lack of constructive mentorship and supportive guidance, or leaders who elevate themselves above those whose skill sets they should be cultivating—these things are as poisonous as open hostility.

It comes down to a single core issue: ego.

Ego is the antithesis of humility. Humility is essential to a healthy creative culture, and ultimately doing our best work. Why? Effective visual communication, intuitive experience design, and functionally engaging front-end development are not subjective. There are clear project goals to be reached and problems to be solved. There is no place for ego there.

When we make ourselves openly available to constructive feedback, we are doing our part to contribute to the ultimate betterment of a piece of work. By checking our egos at the door, we're innately operating in unison instead of hierarchical cliques. I cannot say this more emphatically: **It's good to be humbled.** Being surrounded with incredible talent and immersed in the brilliance of your team is a distinct gift, not a check on your own self-esteem.

In *Egonomics*, David Marcum and Steven Smith note the "cost of ego" on workplace culture:

- *Hearing, but not listening*
- *People thinking "me first, company second"*
- *Only the "right" people have good ideas*
- *Pressure to fit in*
- *Failure to challenge status quo*
- *Candid discussion saved for outside the meeting*
- *Failures being buried and never mentioned again*
- *Silos created and tolerated*
- *Meetings going longer than necessary*
- *Fear of making mistakes or admitting them*

These erosions effectively permeate all office interactions and dynamics: human-centered and project-focused. In a survey for *Egonomics*, Marcum and Smith cited that 63 percent of employees say ego negatively impacts work performance on an hourly or daily basis.

Companies aren't successful based on the initiatives of a single person, humble or otherwise. It takes a motivated, engaged, supported team to help elevate the business.

Psychologist Dr. Maynard Brusman notes in his piece "The Costs of Ego":

"The hardest side of business to master is the human component. Entire industries are now dedicated to providing training and development to organizations challenged by the behavior of their 'human capital.'"

Ego needs to be self-managed, and also noted and corrected as it rears its ugly head. This self-monitoring has to happen daily, in every meeting and every conversation. It's evolution, with the goal being nothing short of crafting the best work possible within the healthiest environment imaginable.

For those in leadership, humility is a quality of paramount importance.

It's effectively impossible for an employee to respect a manager that puts their ego first. The "because I said so" approach our parents may have imbued us with growing up will now only serve to alienate (or piss off). It's the same as when a team or organizational leader "puts their boss hat on" in a dialogue; they can leave the hat on the rack by communicating consistently and clearly. If a team or practice lead is truly operating in your—and the project's—best interest, they'll, in fact, welcome the constructive criticism..

True respect levels the playing field culturally; everyone's voice is valued and an integral slice of the pie. By thinking, working, or communicating in a manner where we're putting ourselves over our teammates, we're immediately marginalizing them as human beings. We're discounting their abilities, ideas, and voice. Respect and collaboration are best friends.

Everyone in a company should have a seat at the table. Jaan Orvet and I chatted about this mindset over coffee while I was writing this book. As he noted:

"To Swedes that comes very easily because it's tied to the whole idea that anyone can share thoughts or ideas. Anyone can collaborate in any process. It doesn't matter how senior or junior you are. It has to do with a bunch of humans coming together to do something, and no human is worth more than another."

Jantelagen.

Successful leadership respectfully guides, augments, supports, and facilitates. I think we've all experienced examples of those who have faltered in that capacity. In a junior role I occupied eons ago, the culture was openly hostile toward mistakes and subjective failure. Whenever I was given the opportunity to present my work to a client, leadership's attitude was one of baited anticipation of any slips I might make (perceived or factual). After wrapping things up, I knew it was a toss-up as to whether management would simply leave the room without ceremony (best case scenario), or if I'd get pulled into any of a handful of Herman Miller-furnished offices for denigration. This type of "leadership" behavior induces anxiety, inhibits confidence, and is tantamount to psychological abuse. No amount of employee compensation validates flaunting your own insecurity.

In contrast, presenting work should always be an opportunity for employees to thrive and succeed. To that end, before any client-facing walkthrough of a project, I give my team some initial thoughts on what we should be covering: "Don't assume the client knows what we know, why we did what we did and what the benefit is to the user and the project's goals." And I clarify our presentation roles: "I'll set the presentation up, and will chime in during your walk-through to supplement your dialogue."

If a team member has a bit less experience and hasn't presented their work before, they need the chance when they feel they are ready. It can start small. On completion, the team can have an open conversation to recap what went well and what needs improvement. If your supervisor isn't putting this together, you and your team most certainly can, very informally. The dialogue here is formed by feedback, not belittlement and threats.

The ultimate goal is exposing everyone to the process of talking through their work, and giving them a (well-supported) chance. Whether in a presentation setting, a code review, or putting design work up on the wall for constructive critique, it's moving toward the same end goal. As team leaders or teammates, we need to support one another in honing our respective crafts. Beyond the betterment of one another and the project at large, this organically generates respect and positivity amongst all involved.

Providing and fostering an environment for open creativity and dialogue is valuable beyond measure: to the overall business, as well as the human-centered energy of the office space. We need to value conversation over oration, collaboration over delegation. People are hired to perform based on their experience and abilities, and acting as a barricade in any capacity is an endless loop of mutually lost opportunity.

Getting out of the Way

Let's think about how user empathy and advocacy is intrinsic to creating optimal user interactions.

Hand in hand with that understanding comes leveraging the

power of humility.

No matter how much knowledge we have accrued and our depth of experience over various projects, we cannot impose a solution on a client simply because we feel it's correct: the user is always right. We test, we refine, we test again, all aimed at creating an organically perfected user experience.

As passionate craftspeople, we can guide and advise, being ever-cognizant of how the user will best achieve their goals. Doing so makes for a better product. It's no ding in our fender to iterate, learn, and evolve. Just as we accept this fact—metaphorically stepping aside to allow user empathy to guide us—we must do the same for the skill sets and abilities of our team members.

We need to make ourselves open to letting our teammates do what they were hired to do. In short, we need to get the hell out of their way and let them shine.

What we find all too often in any business setting where designers and front-enders co-exist is that stakeholders at the team level, or higher in the seniority chain, can (and do) impose constraints throughout the process. Be it from a project's inception, or throughout its entire lifecycle. When there is too much ego in the room, there isn't much space left for creative pursuit.

So then, to our previous thoughts on humility: how does respect toward our team's talent (whether as their manager or their peer) cooperate with enforcing and directing how they should function? Project-wise, client communication-wise, or problem solving-wise?

It does not. Ever. Oil and vinegar, fire and ice, Batman and Joker.

The special sauce here is how project-focused interactions between teammates transpire. There is a fundamental difference between ordering ("It needs to be like this.") and guiding ("Your approach has bold thought behind it, but I wonder if it might be too strong; I'd consider this instead..."). The former is fed by ego, a singular mindset toward visual or programmatic communication. "You're wrong because I'm right." The latter response is predicated upon humility and serves to leverage alternative perspectives. "You're on the right track. What if we tried it this way?"

In terms of the day-to-day, this means not hovering over a teammate (or employee)'s shoulder. Being a victim of back seat directing is belittling and nerve wracking. Involvement-wise, it also means not completely abandoning teammates to flounder without guidance up until the last minute, or at all. There are shades of grey on the spectrum of interaction between smothering and detachment.

Casual check-ins and informal dialogues throughout the day will humanize the experience, giving you the opportunity to talk through any current hang-ups or concerns. A successful dialogue is an open exchange of ideas. It's also a validation of approaches against a project's goals and a user's expectations. Being respectful of an employee's thought processes doesn't mean you shouldn't challenge them, however. It's organic coaching, transparent and respectfully delivered.

In Practice, From England

Some organizations excel at getting out of the way of their talent, and they are extremely passionate about it. Andy Budd and his business partners founded the studio Clearleft in Brighton, England in 2005. As he told me, they formed the agency to be "the kind of place where, if we were employees, we'd like to come into work. But also, to get the right people, we wanted to have a great space."

Over the years, their human-centered initiatives have consistently set them apart as beacons of creative culture. For example, in creating the Open Device Lab concept, allowing colleagues and the public at large into their space to test their digital work on mobile devices. Or in developing Hack Farm, their offsite employee-centric re-energizing retreat.

Widely publicized, their business model and cultural values inherently draw in the right kind of talent: those who have similar values, and also are seeking a truly creative culture in which to do their best work. Clearleft employees have autonomy to operate as not just a dynamic group, but also as proponents and champions of their own work and problem-solving. Andy notes:

"You see really talented designers, really talented developers, really talented UX people, being told, 'you have to do this, because we sold it to the client,' or, 'you can't do that, because we haven't sold it to the client,' or, 'you can't say what you think to the client, because we might lose the contract.'"

There are numerous potential cracks in the foundation of that dynamic. It's likely team members were not included or consulted in the project's inception stage. Hours, features, scope, and/or budget were probably communicated in exclusive conversations. Or, there are stakeholders in the project who are setting design or programmatic direction at their discretion, effectively relegating the brilliance of the team to a production unit. In essence, there are too many cooks in the kitchen, and none of them are the ones who will be making the meal. As Andy told me:

"You're hiring really smart people, and then you're taking away all the opportunity for them to apply those smarts to the problem."

When a designer's creativity has to first be filtered through micro-management or ego, the losses are summarily painful to consider. Team morale is nil; their passions are wasted. Their insights and varied approaches to problem-solving lost. Collective energy is depleted, the project's end goals are compromised, and the end user is lost in the mix of dysfunction.

"How about this crazy idea where we hire smart people, we get out of their way, and then we let them solve the problems," Andy said of his business' model. *"It sounds really simple, but you'd be amazed how few companies do it."*

From Business to Employee

A healthy dynamic between company and employee is established upon the same foundational elements as peer-to-peer, peer-to-team, and peer-to-supervisor. The scale of the interaction rises, but the core values all feel the same.

Within all levels of the seniority chain of any organization, there is a responsibility to support, champion, or engage with the culture so that it can thrive.

Of course, I'm not advocating that business leaders have blinders on toward the bottom line. Nor am I implying that they need to take the focus away from what their role requires. I'm just saying they need to get out of the way of the talented people on their team.

Leaders need to be supporting and enabling managers and team leads to propel and enrich the creative culture on the day-to-day; they in turn must support their employees to have the same level of impact. That responsibility carries throughout the organization, from those who sign the paychecks to those who make the coffee (which can be the same person, sometimes).

People want to come into work, they want to learn and tinker and discover away from the office, and then bring those discoveries and that energy right back into their work and the culture.

Within the office space itself—as in, the physical surroundings—the business' cultural support needs to manifest itself in a tangible way. It can be as simple as some couches set aside in a nook or two for quiet conversation or refocusing: a space that's organic for gathering away from desks, or a coffee machine with some chairs or stools so people can linger for a few minutes if they'd like.

Beware the Perk

Sometimes, a company culture will offer perks that also appear to be wonderful demonstrations of humanity: a quiet sensory depravation-like enclosure for catnaps! A paid service that will come and clean my home, so I don't have to worry about such bothersome tasks! Free cabs home if I'm at the office past 9 PM!

In many cases, these are in fact cultural Band-Aids, and in large part, they're designed to:

1. Make sure you're physically at work as much as possible, and
2. Reframe unhealthy employee expectations as corporate empathy.

Unfortunately, the "sweetness" of these types of perks and how they're marketed (both internally and externally) puts the focus on some very unhealthy behavior.

The thing is, the inherent problem with brilliant employees is that they're by definition, well, *not stupid*. People know when they're being pandered to, or duped, or when they need to put on their knee-high boots. In fact, the only thing worse than not being sincere at all is faking it.

There are some simple, genuine nods toward an open and healthy culture that can come from on high. In company meetings, it's a strong sign of openness and transparency when profits, goals, new business, and operational matters are shared. People like to know what's going on with the company they're supporting.

They also like to feel seen. Appreciated. A gesture toward balancing practical information and human-centered stories can be communicating, say, who's working on an interesting personal project on their own time. Who is giving a talk at a Meetup? Who made a breakthrough in their work earlier in the month? Who deserves a pat on the back for helping out a teammate? Who learned a new skill? How might they integrate that new ability into upcoming projects? Sharing in this way puts a "soul" to the faces you pass in the hallway or bump into at the coffee machine.

Going All In

A healthy dynamic at all levels of an organization forms the backbone of a creative culture. The physical and psychological environment is better equipped to fuel inspiration on a daily basis, and sees the profit in employee growth, not just via the almighty dollar.

This level of investment on behalf of the business means no half measures. Included within that support of employee growth comes a core mindset of how the value of an employee's time is measured.

CHAPTER

3

The
Value
of Time

/ 5

100% billability.

There's a broad notion in our industry that an employee's utilization needs to be at, or near, maximum (business) profitability at all times. It's not uncommon for designers and developers to spend their entire careers under this cultural Sword of Damocles. For those in service organizations, this can mean their merit is quantified by how many line items on their time sheet are client job codes.

This mentality sets the precedent that an employee's worth directly correlates to their tally of completed work. It also effectively crushes any opportunity to harness inspiration. No available time means no time to harness or grow energy; available time is micro-analyzed and frowned upon until it gets filled. It's a cancerous loop.

On the other side of the coin, profitability is not the sole driving factor behind why a company is created, why a project is taken on, or why an employee comes to work each day. Companies *can*, in fact, be "a good place to do good work." That's exactly how Clearleft was conceived and successfully continues to operate today. In fact, many businesses cross-industry are founded upon this humble yet amazing goal; they just lose their soul, and inspired employees, along the way.

To do our best work, to grow our skill sets, and to cultivate an environment in which passions thrive, we first need to stop casting a judgmental eye at "available" time that supports employee growth. We then need to ensure such time is planned for, available, and encouraged in practice.

Challenging the Basic Perception

Clearly, a business relies upon billable hours to function; that's what keeps the lights on. But allowing your employees the time to apply their efforts to other things is important too. There's naturally a balance to be had between securing time for employee development and leveraging it for project goals and deliverables. Some weeks and cycles will afford more time blocks than others. That said, much of the time we'll be discussing here is interlaced organically throughout a workday, instead of conglomerating in large "away from the desk" units. It's quality and usage versus quantity and waste.

What I'm advocating for represents a shift in thinking, a shift in process, and a shift in how we track and value employees' time. As an industry, we've made similar thought and procedural shifts in this capacity before—as in when we began advocating for the user at the discovery level, bringing UX into the forefront of our approaches. Today, it's exceedingly evident that time spent on discovery and UX is vital for a digital project's livelihood; we need to apply that same reevaluation to time spent on employee success.

It's a shift that comes at multiple levels, ultimately. Ownership needs to support and champion the value of growth-based time, and empower managers to enforce the practice procedurally. Project managers and product owners need to ensure such time is consistently planned and allocated for in scheduling. It's one of those things that's easy to neglect—"If we could just put in a little more overtime this week to get ahead of the curve..."—but those decisions ultimately form small cracks in the cultural foundation.

It can start in the smallest of ways: sitting at one's desk, reading an article on programmatic advancements. Hell, sometimes it's nice just to pause for a few moments and catch up on the news. It's less the act of what you're doing, and more about resetting your creative energy through a calm and predictable activity— without worrying about 'getting caught.'

Previously in my career, if I happened not to have a project file open when management walked by, it was a death sentence for my remaining workweek. "Clearly you don't have enough going on right now," I'd be told. The reality was I had plenty of work, but I wasn't doing my best problem solving; I needed a "mind breather," and got summarily chastised for it. You'd walk around the office and see people leaning forward in their chairs trying to shield their screens in stolen moments of un-billability; each of us pitiful in our predicament and posture.

In what amounts to a fraction of a percent of someone's day, we need to communicate (verbally, procedurally, physically) that it's perfectly acceptable to, quite simply, pause. Refresh. Regenerate and renew. Management needs to trust their employees to seize these moments with sincerity and ensure they know they're allowed to do it in the first place.

For employees, especially newly hired ones, having such time made openly available can be a bit of a shock. It's as though we need to be de-brainwashed of what has been expected of us throughout our careers. Unhealthy professional relationships can become our default setting, like a dysfunctional security blanket. It may be a challenging awakening, but it's one that yields a pretty butterfly post-metamorphosis.

> *"Is it ok that I'm sitting on the couch in the lobby right now reading an A List Apart piece?"*

> *"This chat by the coffee machine on the new .js framework is really interesting; I wonder if it's ok to talk it through?"*

> *"I'm having a problem-solving block for some reason today; think it's cool to go out for a walk and reset?"*

The answer to all of the above questions comes from the immortal Heisenberg: You're goddamn right.

Designers and developers, it's your right to have time in your day-to-day for professional development, and it needn't come at the cost of putting food on the table. Being utilized solely as a line-item resource in an Excel spreadsheet is an insult to your passions, evolution, and ability to do your best work. Once we all recognize that we're human beings, the door is open for so many incredible things to happen.

In Organic Interactions

When you're part of a healthy creative culture where both project work and professional development carry equal weight, there are numerous ways in which to harness that energy. It all begins from seizing organic interactions throughout the day.

Let's call it *the act of the linger.* That simplest of gestures—not rushing back to your desk—is one small step for employee, one giant leap for creative culture.

Different office space configurations play their role in how and where organic interactions can present themselves. Sometimes a floor plan is less open, and cubicles or demi-partitioned desks comprise the lay of the land. Or, offices and doors form a physical, barrier, blocking that creative energy from being shared amongst everyone. Rearranging the room may not be an option, so interactions need to be consciously sought out. The responsibility is on everyone to make themselves available: physically by getting up out of their chairs and away from their desks, and mentally by engaging their teammates.

At the office, if I'm eating on premises, I'm not a long lunch kind of guy. It's a personal preference, not a cultural constraint. I'll have some reading material out next to my food, quickly clear my plate while perusing, and clean my place. It may not be the most visually elegant procedure (the crumbs in my beard and aghast coworkers tell the tale), but that's how I enjoy my lunch. Others around me enjoy at a slower pace, chatting and laughing with their friends and co-workers, and letting any negative energy or stress slough off—they are on break after all. Conversations range from current projects to the last episode of a tv show everyone is engrossed in, to an exhibition someone attended over the weekend. Sometimes the dialogue lasts a half hour, sometimes an hour plus. That's how they enjoy their lunch.

Throughout the day, I'll pause by the espresso machine and enjoy a cup. Slowing myself down, tamping grounds into the portafilter to get the right amount of crema; it's a meticulous detail-centric act that produces a tangible (delicious) result. The process calms and refocuses me, despite the fact that I'm by no means an ace barista. Sometimes, I'll have a stand-up with my team around the espresso machine, or ask those I bump into about their day. That's how I enjoy my coffee. Others will come into the kitchen, pop in a single-serve coffee pod, take a sip and head straight back to their chair. That is how they enjoy their coffee.

The point is that there's no right or wrong way to capitalize on those available moments; different things work for different people throughout the day, but there is a definitive common thread no matter what the use case is. Everyone is taking due time in these organic interactions to let the moment stand, and let things unfold organically. In having the cultural opportunity to have such time available without fear, the possibilities for profession-based dialogue, eureka moments, and attacking problems freshly focused are endless. All the while, we're interacting as human beings, creating in an industry that is inherently user-focused.

In Planned Interactions

It's no concession toward a creative culture to have planned moments of interaction throughout the day, or week, to compliment those that organically unfold. In fact, these calendar-secured blocks of time consistently keep the energy flowing. They're a boon. The secret sauce is ensuring such time is optimized for channeling that energy back into their work, and in keeping people mutually motivated.

For example, I run a weekly meeting internally dubbed "Creative Inspiration Wednesdays." It's uncoincidentally situated (US) morning mid-week and serves a very specific purpose. These mornings are intended to start a little bit slower, as the meeting begins at 9:30 AM; there's enough time for a longer breakfast, but not enough time to dive into client work. Again, no coincidence. Between offices from international branches, designers and developers dial in on-time to talk through things that have inspired them over the past seven days.

We share our laptop screens and elaborate on the bits of inspiration we want to share. Low hanging fruit in our industry is a thoughtful website design, or an interesting mobile app interaction, or a book or article someone read on a developing digital trend. Nuggets of inspiration that are directly relatable and applicable to what we're creating daily.

What really generates discussion though are the areas of inspiration that deviate from the digital realm. An online video clip of a documentary on graffiti. An illustrator's body of work. The design of a Bauhaus-inspired Max Bill timepiece (ok, that one was me). We talk through why these areas of inspiration away from the viewport mean something to us; the thought process, how they tackled a problem, or how something specific was achieved through its constraints.

This meeting can last anywhere from 20 minutes to 60 minutes. As the ultimate stakeholder in design and front-end's deliverables in Chicago, I ensure the environment of the call is relaxed, unrushed, healthy, and productive. I'm fully cognizant of—and never lose sight toward—the client-centric work to be accomplished for the day. And so are the call's participants; everyone is fully capable of self-managing their workload to ensure they can have this time for inspiration. Following the call, one of our team members posts the links to a private board for everyone to be able to reference now and in the future.

Our client's work is imperative, of course. But each of us knows it's just as important to have the chance to recharge our energy with inspiration that's cross-medium, cross-culture (and in this instance, I mean between international offices and those in the US), and can be discussed and drawn upon as fuel throughout the remainder of the week.

This fuel serves as a consistent recharge for our creative energy, and in turn, helps the caliber of our work stay consistent. Fuel begets energy; energy begets quality.

The Art of the Fika

Standing "coffee dates," if you will, are also a great way to sync up throughout the day, away from our desks, and recalibrate ourselves. In Swedish culture, there is the concept of *fika*, which means to, more or less, take time out during the day for coffee and a bite to eat. However, it's much deeper than that: it's time to catch up with a friend, to interact as human beings. It's time reserved specifically for taking a break. Fika is such an important thing to Swedes, in fact, that it's often built into employee contracts.

Drift is a magazine that covers coffee culture globally. Their Stockholm edition aptly put it:

"Fika is the thread that weaves Swedish social customs together, and

it's the ultimate nod to the idea of slow living. In our fast-paced world, where we are constantly on deadline or planning our schedules around meetings and events, we crave opportunities to slow down. Swedes actually embrace those opportunities."

When I first observed fika a handful of years ago at the office, watching the Swedes around me get up mid-afternoon daily, stop working, and just...chat over coffee and pastries, I thought I was hallucinating. Are they just talking to one another in the middle of the day? Is that phone going to keep ringing? It took me a good week to allow myself to get up as well and join them; my previous experience as an employee in the US had psychologically shackled me to my chair.

The concept, in practice, is a revelation. Employees have their planned fikas, they meet at various spots in the office during the afternoon, and they take their due time to chat with one another. It's beautiful, it makes perfect sense, and I absolutely cannot imagine having it any other way. The rejuvenation and humanization of the interaction are inarticulable, their value immeasurable. It's a Swedish cultural staple, but any culture can seize its benefit.

In Open Areas

Some locations within an office can be organically conducive to employees congregating for a conversation. As we've discussed, the coffee machine, kitchen area, an employee lounge, all can fall into that bucket. There's also tremendous benefit in designating an area for open thought and creation, without cannibalizing needed workspace.

First, there needs to be a critical delineation made as to what constitutes a space for harnessing and renewing energy. It comes down to the difference between a **distraction** and an **outlet**.

For example, when I was in the early stages of my career and came home from a challenging day at work, I'd turn on my video

FIG 3: TANGIBLE MEDIA CAN RESET OUR CREATIVE PROBLEM SOLVING.

game system and lay the smack down on pixel people in *Street Fighter* for a couple of hours. It'd ultimately be time for bed, yet I was still completely wired and carrying the same negative energy with me that I brought in the door. All I had done was distracted myself. Eventually, I learned that I needed to actually *do something* with that anxiety and stress after work: going for a run, building something, illustrating something, etc.—something healthy, something constructive, and something that afforded actual personal benefit.

Consider an area within the office that encourages employees to work with tangible media, completely out of the context of the digital realm. We're all problem solving during our day: visually, structurally, programmatically. There's immense value in refocusing that process back to making decisions, exploring, building, and experimenting with our hands. I'm not talking about scrimshawing a masterpiece out of a single piece of oak or chiseling a sculpture out of a block of Italian marble. No, I'm talking about Legos. Inkwells and brushes on 80 lb. paper (FIG 3).

3500-piece puzzles.

Jo Cofino's article "Why Lego's CEO Thinks More Grown-Ups Should Play at Work," asks the man behind the bricks, Jørgen Vig Knudstorp, about the value of hands-on play in the workplace. Citing that "one of the biggest mistakes companies can make is to think that sticking a foosball or Ping-Pong table in the office equates to playfulness," Knudstorp noted:

> *"It goes a lot deeper than that, and play offers a lot of promise for businesses. Creative companies create inspiring environments. Tim Brown of innovation and design company Ideo says play creates a risk-free environment that encourages people to experiment, as there is no such thing as failure. It is much more conducive to problem solving than the traditional 'I am right and you are wrong and there is only one way of doing things.'"*

Within an office, does it need to be a planned thing to approach this "play area" and create? It can be, but a developer may also just hop out of their chair, beeline it to the Legos, and start building something with intensity. Perhaps a coworker is there already, building and deconstructing. Some may prefer solitude in creation; others may question, collaborate, and refashion.

TED speaker and psychiatrist Dr. Stuart Brown cites the benefits of this type of motor skill-centric activity for adults in his aptly titled book, *Play*. Agnostic of role, career path, or skill set, he notes that it's more about the voluntary act itself instead of the outcome of the creation. Taking you "out of time," it affords a sense of engagement, augmenting problem solving and creativity.

In Areas Without Walls

For the cost of some art supplies or a trip to the toy aisle at Target, an organization can significantly augment its support of all time with tools for regenerating energy. There's an endless fountain of inspiration to be had away from the psychological container of a desk in a healthy creative culture.

But let's take it a step further and look beyond the confines of the workspace.

To only set our sights on our office space as the sole means of recharging and refueling is to ignore the entire world outside the front door. The personal (and business) value is found in how we leverage the energy obtained away from our desks and infuse it back into our work. A genuine creative culture supports drawing from both indoor and outdoor environments as needed.

4

Beyond
the
Viewport

While our livelihoods exist within the digital realm, inspiration has no such contextual boundaries.

We've discussed outlets, interactions, and moments to be seized while in the physical walls of our work environment. Within those halls is an enormous amount of energy to be harnessed and channeled, but what of the environment we pass through as we make our way into the office?

The Revolution of Stepping Away from Your Desk

There is an entire world of design and inspiration beyond the context the digital world affords us.

Though "thinking outside the box" is a hack term at this point, the sentiment is genuine: the box is our MacBook Pros. The soft ambient glow of a Retina display bathes our faces, its viewport locks our gaze and, in turn, our bodies. "Taking a break" often just means clicking over to a different screen. I'm sometimes guilty of this myself, and the process has a pattern:

- Visual design block hinders momentum.
- "Best of" collections populate a barrage of new browser tabs. This daily winner, that nominee.
- Via minimal effort I've ascertained mass audience-approved web fonts, grid patterns, and content integrations.
- It goes on: responsive navigational system libraries. App UI interaction snippets. All ripe for the picking. My synapses enjoy their coffee break.

Having my viewport blinders on robs me of not just original thinking, but also truly understanding to where my inspiration vanished. Or where it came from in the first place. Quieting our minds is no small feat with the digital world perpetually clawing for our attention. Screens are omnipresent: at our desks, in our pockets, on public transport. It takes attention and effort to reserve time out of their reach, and exertion is always at odds with comfort—and habit, for that matter. Comfort is the bane of advancement.

There are smaller moments in the morning where I simply need to get outside. With the morning's calm, preceding the day's (and clients') awakening. Some days welcome us with inspiration waiting to be seized, to be channeled as fuel as project- centric minutes loom large. Sometimes inspiration requires you to seek it out.

It's at this moment where we need to challenge ourselves.

As with my earlier fika example of initially being "unable" to join my coworkers, this is the definitive point in which we liberate ourselves from those mental shackles. In the drudgery of the post-lunch afternoon, this can manifest in a simple walk around the block. The culture of the office sets the supportive tone here by letting these moments occur unfettered. In one company I worked at previously, I was required to sign out at the reception desk every time I walked out the front door; for lunch, for a breath of fresh air downstairs, for anything. The minutes I tallied, to be made up apples-for-apples upon my return. In this single act, I felt marginalized, scrutinized, and patronized. It provided for a steady stream of head-shaking resentment amongst my co-workers as well.

Trust and Performance

A creative culture openly supports the basic human need to let our minds breathe away from our desks. It lets the energy outside our walls inform the people within. There's demonstrated trust from company to employee in getting out of the way, leaving that door wide open, and not lording over their minutes like Sauron over Mordor. Of course, there's a balance to be had: an employee must also understand that this doesn't mean "take the afternoon off and go on a discovery walk"; something in the ballpark of a half-hour is usually solid. If people feel trusted, they will reward that notion with freshly charged creativity and increased productivity.

The study "Employee trust and workplace performance" published in the *Journal of Economic Behavior & Organization* conducted research on the relationship between employee trust and workplace performance across three variables:

1. The businesses' financial performance
2. Labor productivity
3. Quality of service or product

Across strict measurement criteria, they noted that "higher levels of average employee trust in managers appear to be positively related to workplace financial performance and labor productivity." In terms of quality of service or product, "employee trust is positively associated with being in the 'a lot better than average' category." Put simply: employee trust in management directly translates to high quality of work and company profit.

On the business' end, this trust and support need to be directly communicated to an employee when they're hired. If it comes "through the grapevine" or is passively observed from afar, the notion that they can just take a break outside might be perceived as suspect or only for a privileged few. Even in a culture that's known for its employee and growth-centered climate, this has to be an absolute known quantity from Day One.

Government Digital Services (GDS) in the UK, which specializes in "the digital transformation of the government," goes as far as to physically post on a wall a list of exactly what their employees can seize, culturally. The "unofficial stuff," as they've dubbed it. Noting things "it's ok to do," such as "go somewhere else to concentrate" or "not check email after hours," employees new and old are crystal clear on the wonderful, oft-unspoken, benefits their culture has to offer. Simple gesture, long-term impact.

On Foot

In the spirit of seizing cultural benefits, let me show you what I do when my inspiration is lacking. I'll draw my example from a morning I had not to long ago.

Heading out the front door as others walk in, I'm also exiting a state of stagnation. As I breathe in fresh air, I'm making myself available to an influx of new energy; I move, and I observe. Am I looking for something that will directly translate to the digital space? No. Perhaps the way a sign painter across the street painstakingly applies letterforms will influence my web typography, or the way a tree branch buckles under a landing bird will inform a web animation, but I'm not banking on it. In eureka moments, direct relations can happen. Such events are gifts, but the intent here is much broader.

Sensory interactions both grand and intimate are longing to be harnessed, processed as fuel. From my company's Chicago location on this morning, I ventured East with subconscious intent toward the Loop. Casting my gaze upward, architecture carved its place in the sky. Refocusing on the bustle before me, a commuter walking in quick step thoughtfully paused to lend directions to a tourist. "The First Time I Met the Blues" poured forth from a street musician's American Deluxe. Ingenuity, humility, and soul were the reward for my half-hour journey. Our human-centered jobs need to consistently be inspired by the very humans we're creating for.

The digital realm is seductive. As problem solvers—simply as users ourselves—we're ever drawn to its lure. Stepping away from "the box" is all it takes to begin a thought shift toward the value of out-of-office inspiration.

In Curated Environments

The inspiration we're able to cull from the world outside our office's front door is in large part "moment-specific," if you will: the interactions, observations, and experiences we happen upon can and will vary based on an endless degree of chance and circumstance. That spontaneity, and the variety it presents, is a large part of its value.

On the other side of the coin, visiting a thoughtfully curated environment where someone has keenly and specifically thought of every detail affords a different, tangible inspiration. One that's deliberately planned and innately consistent.

Our field requires we give empathetic thought to the implications of every decision we make. We're creating interactive experiences for humans that serve to be as functional, usable, and intuitive as possible. At the same time, we're considering the value of every detail and the role it plays in the quality of the end product. This is where the synergy of inspiration between the digital and physical realms functions to our advantage.

Beauty in the Details

The Soho House group has hospitality-focused properties spanning Europe and North America. Designed as a space for "creative souls" to inspire and be inspired, the brand is known for its thoughtful fusion of industrial design, elegance, and comfort in its décor, furnishings, and art. Letting the respective building's history and geographical location keenly inform the creative process, the painstaking craft of this marvelous balance is driven by resident Design Director Vicky Charles. As she noted in *Better Interiors:*

> *"Our design is very much led by and sympathetic to the local environment. We always work with custom design furniture and antiques but we respect the original finishes and architecture of the space, so each property is different."*

The Chicago House is walkable from my home or office, and one I often frequent for haircuts, coffee, or writing (including the section you're reading right now). Not only is every property unique, but each room in every property also has no duplicate; spanning the 40 quarters in this building, that's a non-trivial feat. The structure—originally The Chicago Belting Factory—leverages much from its own history, as well as the city's past, toward its present incarnation.

The structurally unsound water tower on the building's roof was deconstructed and repurposed as a mural in the lobby. The blue tone employed on the exterior awnings, with full intention, matches original paint that was discovered in the warehouse. Chicago's last remaining tannery, Horween Leather, lent their craftsmanship to the gym's equipment.

Sitting on the Club Floor over a cup of coffee, there's an energy to the space that's fueled by these thoughtful details. They factor right down to the curve of the coffee cups and writing-conducive workspaces. These little unobtrusive rewards elicit positive emotional responses; they're complimenting my experience of writing or just defusing. As in my digital, experiential work, the very same positive emotional responses gained through thoughtful user interactions compliment my (user) journey.

To Caffeine and Beyond

It's no secret that people gravitate to coffee shops to work, read, or catch up with a friend. Like Soho House's Club Floor, many coffee shops afford what *The Atlantic's* Conor Friedersdorf calls, "just enough distraction." That is to say, enough noise to break the harsh silence of an office environment, but not at live concert levels. Cafés can make for a phenomenal alternative for doing charged work away from our desks, especially when the environment is a deliberate, curated space conducive to creative energy.

My team at work has full reign to design and code agnostic of workspace; around the office proper, that freedom is well-utilized. There's still an apprehension to do so away from the office. So engrained are we to stay within our physical walls during business hours that I've actually had to make it a **requirement** that my team picks a café to work from one morning a week. Without having chatted about it beforehand, I later discovered Jaan Orvet did the same imposed coffee shop trip with his team over in Sweden. Psychological shackles of unhealthy cultures past have no geographic boundaries.

The selection of which coffee shop to work from isn't an arbitrary one. Via peer dialogues and online reviews we do our homework in advance, ascertaining how conducive a potential space is to curated inspiration and seizable energy. One such long-time favorite is Heritage Bicycles General Store, in Chicago's Lakeview neighborhood. Founded by Michael and Melissa Salvatore, Heritage is equal parts custom bike manufacturer (the first in the city since 1982) and ultra-curated café. In an open floor plan intentionally designed to generate energy and conversation via its seating arrangement (mostly communal), the "placement with purpose" interior decorating offers plenty of spatial inspiration.

The ol' typewriter, handcrafted reclaimed wood table, and coffee shop combo may scream "hipster," but for our intents and purposes that's an association I'm quite comfortable with. The hipster-driven "handcrafted" movement gets its share of sneers, but at its heart is a passion for craft: through coffee shops, niche clothing stores, or farm-to-table restaurants. In that way, be it through the lens of beans or selvedge denim or pork shoulder, there's a deliberate and focused nature that fuels the selection of elements down to a microscopic level of detail. Quality in the end product defines the goal of the process.

Over the years, via syncing up with Orvet in Stockholm for our standing coffee chats, we often continue our dialogue outside with specific stops in mind. Sometimes, it's been a denim boutique on the island of Södermalm. Other times, a brilliantly stocked magazine shop. One such example of the latter has been Papercut, who's ambition is "to create the ultimate store for people who consider fashion, art, literature, design, film, music, etc. an important part of their lives." Its scope and scale have been daunting to me in the times I've had the opportunity to browse.

That said, the sheer quantity of material has not come at the sake of its careful selection; the shop is magnificently curated. At the various companies with which Jaan has done his experience-based work, he's brought his team to Papercut, mid-workday, often. As he noted about one such excursion:

"The decision to go there was to spend an hour in a nicely curated environment where the people that work there can answer a question about any title. (It's about) being in an environment where someone has thought about every aspect, because that's what we need to do. So, instead of talking about the importance of quality, going to a quality place to pick up magazines is a way of bringing it into day-to-day life."

Hackathons and Retreats

There are many companies out there who offer professional development-based perks to their employees: online courses, association memberships, and industry conference trips among them. For example, when I was with Nansen the conference trip option was already a part of their cultural offering; something I keenly considered as I weighed my options.

The one stipulation was that, upon an employee's conference return, they present back to the company what they got out of the opportunity and the (potential) worth to other team members in attending next year. Not a bad deal, right? It's a strong demonstration that employees are seen as much more than instruments of client project execution, and showed that we wanted our team members to grow and evolve.

Inspiration acquired from conferences in our industry can be quite valuable: you're listening to thought leaders present on tech trends, their professional experience, and insights into where design and development are headed. Beyond an overall sense of being recharged and re-energized toward our crafts, the end goal is to hopefully infuse this new learning back into our daily work and active projects.

When you're in a seat at a conference, it's called **passive learning**. By and large, you're not so much engaging with the material and speaker as much as absorbing nuggets of wisdom. Focusing on a notepad to jot down a resonated thought or grabbing a mobile device to tweet a sound bite serves as a pervasive distraction against the overall experience. You're being talked at from afar, with the dynamism of conversational exchange lost.

Active Learning

We can do more toward the benefits obtained by sending someone to a conference, and at a fraction the cost. Let's consider the spirit of a **hackathon** instead.

At the highest level, a hackathon encourages a group of people to create (programmatically *and* visually, ideally) in unison and produce something amazing together, typically over the course of a few days or weekends. This partnered problem solving builds a shared creative energy that lasts well beyond the event's conclusion. It's why so many people love to participate.

It's this idea—of people coming together, creating something amazing without the constraints of the context of client work—that inspired Clearleft to start their Hack Farm concept.

Beginning in 2011, and repeated annually since, the entirety of their agency has come together as a single team to build something unique and fun. Having rented a farmhouse away from the buzz of the city for their inaugural event, and going into it without a plan of what to hack, they came away with Map Tales, a tool to help people tell stories illustrated with maps.

I tried to push Andy Budd a bit to ascertain how challenging it was for their company to shut down operations for a week, put projects and deliverables on hold, and trek into rural England to get away from it all. Despite my prodding, the fish weren't biting. There was no challenge, no trepidation, he explained; it was the most natural thing in the world for them to do.

"We wanted to do it as a retreat or an escape from commercialization. We went in with the idea that whatever we built wasn't going to be a thing. We don't want to launch it and ship it and make millions. We want to have a bit of fun. We want to explore new ways of thinking, new ways of working."

And though Clearleft is a mid-size company, size isn't a limiting factor toward the same cultural support. Twitter's quarterly internal Hack Week has yielded everything from practical functionality like the ability to archive your own tweets to the more fanciful open-source photo-tweeting birdhouse. Many organizations have seen the value of these types of internal retreats; the wins, they are aplenty.

Leveraging Clearleft's Hack Farm as our model, my friend and colleague Andreas Carlsson and I started a program a few years back called Wintercamp. With the very goal of fostering active-over-passive learning, everyone in the business—all roles from our global locations—was invited to centralize at a retreat in rural Sweden to create something together. The process of what we'd build was a learning process: too pre-planned (going in with designated options) at first, and then not planned enough (going in and figuring it out on-site). And ultimately, as in Little Red Riding Hood's porridge, just right: a couple "tracks" (ideas, more broadly) over a few very fluid teams.

We developed tools we could use in our daily process once back on home turf. We'd participate in open collaboration and non-adversarial discussion. We put faces to names of people only previously known from an email chain. Our titles were irrelevant; the teams we formed, flat and collegial.

When participants weren't focused on work, they'd cook for one another, have endless discussions about their mutual craft(s), and enjoy the surrounding expansive grounds and leisure activities. At the end of each day, the various project teams would present to each other what they've accomplished, what the pitfalls were, and solicit open and honest feedback.

People returned to their home offices recharged. Invigorated and inspired by their global coworkers, they acted as living embodiments of the culture. The projects worked on at Wintercamp continued as formal entities once we were back at our desks, which kept the momentum going. And teams functioned more effectively, having worked toward common goals and made deeper personal connections.

All Work and No Play Makes Jack a Dull Boy

The rural environment in which Wintercamp is held is a deliberate selection, conducive to outdoor enjoyment and activities that promote humanizing the experience. That said, the start-up atmosphere of Wintercamp had often compromised our participants actually *getting outdoors*. People had become so charged from creating that they've rarely left the cabin.

And so, Carlsson and I reevaluated the experience and turned it into something else. Enter [x]Camp.

[x]Camp was conceived specifically to get people interacting with their environment and thinking away from their laptops. To have them rethink problems and solutions by utilizing their surroundings, and to have those surroundings supply maximum, unending inspiration.

I secured the Hauer Ranch in Moab, Utah, just minutes from Arches National Park (Fig 4), to provide exactly such an experience. With a dozen co-workers distributed between three SUV's, we hashed out some rough themes to work on over the 4-hour drive from Salt Lake City down to Moab. Inclusive of the benefit of its surroundings and isolation, the Ranch was also selected because its Wi-Fi connection was, as advertised, passable at best. Basic browsing and email checking were about as involved in the digital world as we could get. And that was the point.

Day One consisted of a five-hour guided hike in the national park's aptly named Fiery Furnace (Fig 4.1) to reset our thinking, set the tone for the camp, and let the environment refuel us. Over the following three days developers sketched database diagrams in the crimson Utah dirt, stand-ups were held upon ancient stone cliffs, and passionate dialogues evolved over wee-hour campfires.

This is a company culture extending its boundaries beyond its walls. It's a tangible demonstration of support and respect that an elevator pitch could never deliver.

Via thoughtful planning, lots of research, and trial-and-error, Carlsson and I developed two ongoing internal camps that have became a staple to the company's identity. People I'd interviewed

Fig 4: Arches National Park, Moab, Utah.

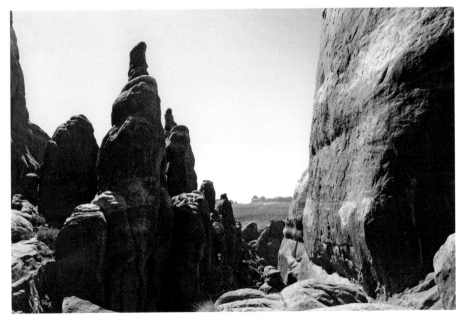

Fig 4.1: The Fiery Furnace, Arches National Park, Moab, Utah.

for roles on my team while at that company had directly cited the camps as the reason they reached out. This positive outward and inward buzz is invaluable, but when it comes down to brass tacks, at what cost does this all come to the company which ultimately foots the bill?

Well, if a business uses the thought of "costliness" as a demerit against the act of sending employees to conferences, I can tell you this about our camps: they come in at about 1/3 the cost, per person, in a comparative sense. By doing advanced logistical planning, centralizing a location to stay, and cooking for one another on a daily basis, costs are mitigated drastically. We've held our versions abroad and within the States, but the duration, scale, and activities can always be adjusted to suit a designated budget.

When the Sun Isn't Shining Over Utah

The tactics, mindsets, organizational shifts, and operational flexibility discussed in this book are predicated upon a simple truth: a company presently supports and operates as a creative culture, or is genuinely willing to evolve to become one.

Having said that, reality isn't always unicorns and rainbows.

For example, the fabric of a company's creative culture can become irreparably frayed due to management changes, acquisition, or it can lack sustainability. Whether these circumstances reveal themselves over years or overnight, your passion and evolution should never be their casualty.

Sometimes, creating within an environment that's the best fit for your growth and passions means finding a new opportunity.

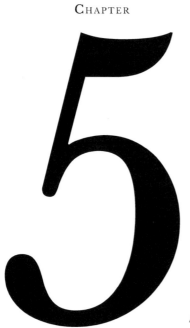

Your Cultural Match

/ 5

Ending an unhealthy relationship is a painful endeavor.

It's an experience many of us have likely had at some point. In a divorce, there's a division of assets and the loss of years of investment. In a break-up, there's the acknowledgment that the honeymoon period wasn't indicative of a long-term, sustainable fit. The experience is rife with disappointment and letdown when reality hasn't met expectations. The same can be said for the moment you look around your workplace and realize: "I've got to get out of here."

Finding your cultural best fit isn't a swipe-left or swipe-right matchmaking process. It requires research, patience, and honesty about your goals, desires, and work habits. As a passionate, dedicated, hungry individual looking to grow and thrive, you deserve nothing less than your perfect cultural match.

There's no "easy way" covered in this chapter. As with everything else we've covered, the mindset of putting humans first—in this case, you—will serve as our compass while navigating new career options.

We began this book with a healthy, human-centered, engaging Day One. Now, we'll conclude by revisiting it, albeit under different circumstances: those that begin to sound your internal alarm.

One Small Step for Gain

As with the Apple onboarding example cited in Chapter 1, there are hallmarks of a first day in any role that can be considered "standard welcoming gestures": intro handshakes and name exchanges. Going out for lunch with your new peers (and not footing the bill). New hardware and some swag. Broadly, these are nice nods toward a potentially solid culture.

Conversely, as I noted earlier through some of my personal experiences on first days, there can be some fairly immediate overt signs of deeper, culturally problematic issues. Getting lobbed into a project within minutes of being on premises. Having no one, save for the person who hired you, aware of your arrival. Cots near the cubicle farm (and people still in them).

As such, we need to take a look at how to react in the instance the culture appears to be not what it seemed initially. Why didn't the company's actual methods (symptoms) come up during the interview process? Did they hide the cots last week? You'd done your homework on the company, had some good dialogue leading up to this point; where did things go astray?

As stressful as first days can unfortunately be, you need to distinguish between the Day One jitters and your gut's revulsion against legitimate red flags. When targeting potential new opportunities, did you seek out this company because of their external brand? Or was it due to what you knew of their internal culture? Dynamic brands and dynamic creative cultures do not always go hand in hand.

Let me tell you about the Day Five Principle, or "Why Every Recruiter in the Galaxy Will Loathe Me Momentarily (#WERGWLMM)."

Let's say your first day has yielded some warning signs that are keenly opposed to your ability to do your best work. Without being overly reactionary, and presuming the best of your new employer, sometimes there are days when things just don't sync up. Like any individual human being, offices or teams can also have bad days where things are out of whack with the overall creative energy and in responding to client needs. For this, let's take some calming breaths, fall into our Jedi peace, and give the company the benefit of the doubt for a standard business week: through Day Five.

Over the course of these five days, and beyond the already noted obvious signs of an unhealthy culture, watch how your teammates interact with one another and with your team leader. Is there a dialogue, or a monologue? Observe what people are doing to collaborate, energize, and inspire one another. If you're ascertaining a grim outlook on those things, or if time given to due process in design and development is relegated to being reactionary to line items on a project brief, the company's creative culture may not be the best fit.

Much of the above can be directly inquired about during your initial conversations and the interview process to mitigate any surprises come Day One and ensure the best cultural fit. We'll look at this process shortly.

There's a grand work up to having taken a new role. That is to say, you've told your friends, your family, maybe taken to social media to let followers know, etc. From this Day One-onward, there's now a steady paycheck en route. Likely some health insurance. Perhaps some sort of 401k. All of these things considered, there is no greater barometer in existence for the reality of your situation and the culture of the new organization than your gut. I don't take it lightly in the least when I say this: it's far better to sever ties quickly than to languish in a situation you absolutely know is wrong for you. Put more directly: get the hell out of there.

I realize what I'm advocating could earn me a few guffaws: "well, you can't do that!" And to that, my response is, well why not? At this point, you have built up momentum in marketing yourself to potential employers. You have your job listing web sites and industry contacts very recently "in play" on your behalf. The ultimate decision comes down to this: having an hour of potential awkwardness in a conversation with HR or a manager, or staying with a company for weeks, months, or years because you feel indebted or socially required. The gesture is also a wake-up call to the organization; your candor, an ice bucket boon to their culture and potentially the other disillusioned employees.

Anything that has culturally revealed itself so clearly in the first five days is a gift to you, your craft, your dignity, and your passion. In unhealthy cultures, sometimes these signs can take time to evolve. Before negativity becomes the norm, and the norm becomes comfort, the freshness of what's transpiring is, in fact, your ally. It makes it easier to see, to assess, and to ultimately challenge what you're willing to accept.

Thinking Outside the Job Board

When you've found a creative culture that reveals itself as a lightning rod for your programmatic or design passion, you'll experience butterflies. Goosebumps. It needn't take having been burned previously in other roles, or on other Day One's, to know deep down that you've found something special. Your gut will plainly tell you this, too.

Your cultural match is out there. Unless you've got an "in" via your network and have a streamlined research and hiring experience, however, it's going to take effort to find it. Just as a creative culture applies human-centered ways of thinking that redefine "standard" business processes, I ask that you shift your way of thinking toward a human-centered, "non-standard" job search.

I'm not going to tell you how to use a job board or list out ways to start a dialogue with a recruiter. While of course incredibly valuable in your process, those are the lowest hanging of fruits on the career hunt tree.

Identify some companies you would love to work with and begin to investigate their story and the way they tell it. How do you feel they portray themselves? What seems most important to them? How do they speak about their people and their work? Which of those (people, or work) have preferential hierarchy in the navigation on their website?

Whether visually or in content, the quality of a company's body of work (product or service-based) is an obvious, readily ascertainable thing. The story behind the work is where their culture comes to light. At what cost was the work created? Was it collaboratively produced? Were the project constraints realistic? Was it via all-nighters for days or weeks on end at the expense of time for recharging or seeing their families?

Many job boards offer Yelp-style reviews of businesses from their past and current employees, providing a sampling of some "behind the curtains" cultural revelations. While helpful, there's a narrative behind the narrative there, and you're only ever going to get part of it with online research.

To truly grasp what the culture of a company you have an interest in is like, let's put it to the test right from the start: via human contact.

Reaching Out

In this role-seeking process, I'm encouraging you to try new avenues of contact and investigation. Passively lobbing a resume and cover letter over the digital fence does not do your passions, your voice, or your rightful place in a creative culture any semblance of justice.

Reach out to the business. Talk to them.

Companies largely have a "Contact" link in their global navigation, yes? Let's put that content to work. Find an appropriate person: General contact? Hiring manager? The person you suspect might work within the discipline in which you're interested? Reaching out over the phone affords ever-vital human interaction and is preferred; email provides the recipient time to respond if they're busy. If the job posting had a "No phone calls, please" qualifier, respect that; it's not a reveal against anything cultural. The responsible party for hiring simply may not be able to take copious calls throughout the course of their day.

"But what if they don't respond? What if they hang up, or shut the door in my face, or it compromises my chances?" you might ask.

Should any of the above occur, what you gain is an immediate insight into their culture, and how it treats other human beings (and potential colleagues). Jaan Orvet told me about an applicant who was looking into a company he recently worked with:

"At the place I was recently with, we talked to a designer who really cares about culture. She was more than welcome to talk to people who have left (the company), and people who are presently employed there. And our clients. It can't be any other way."

If you have the opportunity after establishing a dialogue with an organization you've reached out to, talk to people who have left the company, at varying levels of hierarchy. If a culture is transparent and the business treats its people with respect, there's nothing to sweep under the rug. They'll appreciate that you care that much and won't hesitate to put you in contact with people that have left.

Knock Knock

The value of reaching out to a company of interest through phone or email is that, no matter the response, you'll learn something valuable about their culture.

Sometimes, there is no contact information available. Sometimes, you have no one "on the inside" vetting a business' culture or expediting your resume's routing process. To the human connection, and in ascertaining "a day in the life" of a business candidly, this can be opportunity rather than roadblock:

How about knocking on their door?

"There was one place in particular where I didn't even remotely know anyone who had something to do with the company. I just went and rang the doorbell, and they opened. I thought I'd see: do they open the door? Who opens the door? And they thought I was really weird, so they let me in."

Orvet was intrigued about a UK business' culture, as he was considering them as an option for a new role. Outwardly, the company had an image of being somewhat cold, despite the tremendous work they produced; he sought to understand the face behind the curtain.

"Just from (ringing the doorbell), they understood something about me, and I thought it was kind of cool when I found out it was one of their senior project managers who opened the door. Everyone there took care of things around the office, opening the door, answering the phone, washing the dishes. They talked to me about why they had the image of being inaccessible. I learned so much."

Ultimately, through a thoughtful 20-minute conversation the employee had with him, it was clear to both sides that there wouldn't have been a cultural match. The fairytale ending to the story would have been that the company opened the door, there was an instant synergistic cultural love affair, and a job offer was extended at minute 21. That's not realistic, nor is it the point of knocking in the first place.

The gesture of a business opening the door and chatting with you is an excellent demonstration of a human-centered belief system. If they slam the door in your face (metaphorically...), you know you don't want to work there. Of course, the company might not be able to talk much at that point but get a sense for what they're doing. Listen to what they're saying. Do they think it's great that you turn up and you're showing initiative? Or, do they say "Oh no, you're the 12th person today to show up. I'm sorry, this doesn't work here."

Well, great: you've learned something about the business and their culture that a job posting cannot provide. Simply by knocking on the door.

The Mutual Interview

Be it via job application, follow-up phone call, or on-site conversation, an interview always comes before signing on the dotted line. This interview is a mutual one to determine an ultimate cultural—and needs—fit: company to you, and you to them.

There will the staple questions: talking through your background, experience, and body of work. "How much notice would you need to give to your current employer (if you're presently employed)?" "Tell me about an area you feel you need improvement?"

(As a side note to the last question: should that one come up, ultimately reflect it back to the business. Transparency would yield a genuine answer in return.)

Those stock questions have their business value. But, you also have to consider what's not being asked. Have you been asked about who inspires you in what you do? How you maintain that inspiration, or convey it to your team? What you read to stay on top of your craft's evolution? How often you attend (or speak at) events, lectures, or meet-ups?

The above speak to passion. To energy. To personal and team-based evolution. A creative culture cares deeply about these things.

My friends, this conversation is where you must dig deep. Be thoughtfully tenacious. In advance of the interview, pick a few things that are of utmost importance to you and to doing your best work. For example, the ability to work offsite. Or, how employees are onboarded. Make sure that those are the things you spend plenty of time asking questions about.

You: *"Do people work from coffee shops?"*
Business: *"Of course!"*
You: *"That's great to hear. Which ones? How long are they able to work there? Are there any particular days they can't do that? Why?"*

If you ask about how you'd be welcomed into the company and culture on your first day, do they have an immediate, detailed, and passionate retort? If the question gets met with stumbles, shrugged shoulders, or flop sweat, that part of their process is likely not thoughtfully cared for.

Keep Your Head on a Swivel

Beyond this dialogue, consider the fact that a "day in the life" of the respective company is effectively unfolding before your eyes at that point, plainly and openly. The spatial observations during an interview are equally paramount to establishing a cultural connection.

If you're not offered a tour of the office, ask to be shown around. What can you spot in the space? We all exercise hyper self-awareness during an interview: *Was that handshake too hard? Am I speaking slowly enough? Do I have salad in my teeth?* Once in the offices of a company you're interested in, however, give equal awareness to your surroundings.

We're talking about basic human observation. Are people having conversations over coffee? Are they scuttling off to meeting rooms? Collaboratively sketching or whiteboarding? Are they smiling? Are they sullen? Take heed of these snapshots as a collective sampling, and compare that picture against the company's story and what you've ascertained from your interview conversation.

Being ever-cognizant of what's important to you to do your best work, take in what you see of the workspace and office layout, too.

Ask questions about what you observe. Are there places for people to work away from their desks? Is management seated in offices or with everyone else? Is there an area for people to creatively reset their energy? As with the interview conversation, probe deeper about what's most important to you.

The Mutual Win

The interview process is for pragmatic investigation. You've made it to the point of having a discussion, and the dialogue you'll be having is exactly that: a conversation, not an interrogation. Use this time to be thoughtful, observant, inquisitive, and above all else, true to yourself and the passion for your craft.

And this is what it's really all about in the end: you. Your work is an extension of yourself. Your **best** work will come from the support and challenge a creative culture will consistently provide you.

Conclusion

Don't settle.

Take your Sunday evenings back; they can exist without anxiety. It can be a night of anticipation of the week ahead, and revisiting the previous one in your mind with the humble recognition of what you accomplished.

Don't settle.

Instead of looking back on years of compromised work and industry burnout, seek out the companies who are doing it right. They're out there. The passion for doing your best work is too precious to be extinguished by an unhealthy culture. The human beings on the receiving end of the experiences we're crafting can't settle for anything less.

Don't settle for a hushed voice. For ego. For a well of inspiration that's perpetually dry.

For many companies and individuals, perceptual and procedural shifts abound in this book. For businesses, how employee time is tracked and measured. For employees, harnessing the tangible to inspire the intangible. Jantelagen puts human-centered interactions at the center of company culture, and it's that mindset of humility and equality that brings us out of the dark ages of the worker as an undervalued production machine.

Across quality of work, quality of culture, and quality of life, the result is nothing short of industry transformation.

About the Author

Justin graduated from The School of the Art Institute of Chicago at a time when the job title "Web Designer" was an ethereal mystery to our moms and dads. With Josef Müller-Brockmann and user advocacy claiming equal parts of his creative heart, he's crafted digital experiences for clients like Sony, Chase, SRAM, IBM, and the U.S. Department of Energy.

Through bloodshot tunnel vision, he's drawn from those career experiences across agency side, client side, design studio, and pure tech to foster healthy, dynamic, supportive creative cultures.

In his miniscule spare time he endlessly pursues side projects over a variety of media; pixel design, and the inherent constraints of the medium, has long been near and dear to his bit-based heart. He founded The Dead Pixel Society with some of the world's best icon designers to carry on that tradition. His published written work has covered everything from usability in video games to the value of coffee toward inspiration.

Justin lives in Chicago with his family. He can happily tell you where to get the best Old Fashioned or chain-stitched selvedge denim in the city.

pseudoroom.com
@pseudoroom

photo by Mark Rowland

Acknowledgements

Above all else, inarticulable gratitude to my wife Kaity for the room to write, think, and to stare into space blankly when cohesive thoughts proved elusive. Keeping our two year-old happily amused and engaged for hours on end while I toiled away on this book is a gift I'm ever-grateful for.

Massive appreciation to my friend and colleague Jaan Orvet for the ever-dependable ear, brilliance, and confidence; truly the Yoda of human-centered creative culture (in wisdom and Force knowledge, not stature or age).

Jeffrey Zeldman's council, candor, trust, and respect proved the impetus for this project; from its humble origins as an *A List Apart* article through a self-published work. Katel LeDu and Lisa Maria Martin provided absolutely invaluable structural and tone-of-voice guidance at the onset of writing, tightening my work and broadening my thinking then and onward. Anne Maynard's wit, editorial genius, and stunning insights brought this book from the minor leagues to the big show.

The copious conceptual brainstorming sessions with Bobby Price were creative fuel for the soul. His illustrative work and raw talent legitimately brought this book to life.

Andreas Carlsson, my brother in design from Linköping, endlessly opened my mind, challenged me to think bigger, and called me on my bullshit (with much appreciation and necessity). Nansen introduced me to Swedish culture in business—and in lifestyle—both in Chicago and Stockholm; experiences and opportunities that had value beyond measure. Ben Cox, my brother from the South, kindly introduced me to Nick Sarillo.

I'm beyond thankful to Nick for the window into his business, humble genius, and incredible story. In tandem, without hesitation the brilliant Andy Budd lent his industry defining thoughts and insights for this book; his cultural initiatives have been cornerstone inspirations. These gentlemen selflessly donated their time and energy to me and this topic due to their collective passion for human-centered work environments, and people being treated fairly and respectfully.

In a tactile sense, my iPad Pro proved to be the ultimate tool for wordsmithing, sketching concepts, and toting to my favorite cafés. High five, Apple. And to those emporiums of caffeine and tranquility whose seats I warmed for hours on end, big ups to Soho House, Hero Coffee, Dollop, Star Lounge, and Standing Passengers.

Lastly, thank you to the city of Chicago, my birthplace and home, for serving up unending inspiration through art, music, and culture. Functioning as the backdrop for much of this book's content and interactions, I can't imagine having written it in any other place.

References

Chapter 1

Inside Apple by Adam Lashinsky
https://www.amazon.com/Inside-Apple-Americas-Admired-Secretive-Company/
dp/145551215X

Chapter 2

Egonomics by David Marcum and Steven Smith
https://www.amazon.com/egonomics-Makes-Greatest-Expensive-Liability/
dp/1416533273

"The Costs of Ego" by Dr. Maynard Brusman
https://www.scribd.com/document/137063530/The-Costs-of-Ego

Chapter 3

Drift Volume 4: Stockholm
https://driftmag.com/products/volume-4-stockholm

"Why Lego's CEO Thinks More Grown-Ups Should Play at Work"
by Jo Cofino in *The Huffington Post*
http://www.huffingtonpost.com/entry/lego-and-the-power-of-play-to-transform-
business_us_55d72809e4b020c386de52bd

Play by Dr. Stuart Brown
https://www.amazon.com/Play-Shapes-Brain-Imagination-Invigorates/
dp/1583333789

Chapter 4

"Employee trust and workplace performance" by Sarah Brown, Daniel Gray, Jolian McHardy, and Karl Taylor in the *Journal of Economic Behavior & Organization*
http://www.sciencedirect.com/science/article/pii/S0167268115001365

"It's ok to say what's ok" by Giles Turnbull on the Government Digital Service blog
https://gds.blog.gov.uk/2016/05/25/its-ok-to-say-whats-ok/

"Old Faithful" by Sheena D'lima in *Better Interiors*
http://www.betterinteriors.in/old-faithful-2/902/

"Working Best at Coffee Shops" by Conor Friedersdorf in *The Atlantic*
http://www.theatlantic.com/business/archive/2011/04/working-best-at-coffee-shops/237372/

cultivating a Creative culture

the-culturebook.com

The book's online home features the Creative Culture podcast of conversations with thought leaders and cultural beacons. The site also houses the Creative Culture blog, the latest news, links, and more.

@the_culturebook

www.the-culturebook.com

@the_culturebook

CPSIA information can be obtained
at www.ICGtesting.com
Printed in the USA
LVIC06n1513130517
534303LV00001B/6

* 9 7 8 0 6 9 2 8 4 0 6 7 2 *